HABITATS

P O E M S

GARRETT ASHLEY

LOBLOLLY PRESS   ASHEVILLE, NC

LOBLOLLY◦PRESS

Published by Loblolly Press
loblollypress.com
Asheville, NC
Copyright © 2026 by Garrett Ashley

All rights reserved. No part of this publication may be reproduced, distributed, or transmitted in any form by any means, including photocopying, recording, or other electronic methods without the prior written permission of the author, except in the case of brief quotations embodied in reviews and certain other noncommercial uses permitted by copyright law. For permission requests, write to the publisher at loblolly.publishing@gmail.com.

Cover design by Lib Ramos
Interior design by Andrew Mack
Instagram: @loblolly_press
Newsletter: loblollypress.substack.com

Paperback ISBN: 979-8-9943089-0-5
Printed in the United States of America

First Printing, April 2026

CONTENTS

I   *[Anomalies]*

The Clams—5
Voices Of The Dead—8
Pine Memories I—10
Pine Memories II—12
December—13
Ghost Balloon—15
Water Noise—16
Spirits Of North America—18
One Way I Am Able To Remember My Mother—20
Trapdoor—22
Year Of Basketball—23
Somedays I Go Missing, And Gilligan Pretends To Be Me—24

II   *[A Field Guide to North American Trees]*

American Holly—31
Balsam Poplar—34
Red Spruce—36
Jack Pine—38
Ginkgo —40
Live Oak—42
Loblolly Pine—44
Poison-Sumac—46
Sweetgum—48
Longleaf Pine—50
Slash Pine—52
Tree Of Life—54
Crape Myrtle—56
Red Juniper (Eastern Redcedar)—58
American Sycamore—60
Southern Magnolia—62

PRAISE FOR GARRETT ASHLEY

"From the very start, Garrett Ashley casts a surreal, imagistic spell that pulls the reader in. These poems offer brief moments to breathe before drawing us back again. Habitats is a book in which to become lost and transformed, and one I will read again and again."
SCOTT OWENS, First Poet Laureate of Hickory, NC, and author of twenty-four poetry collections, including Elemental

✻

"With Habitats, Ashley creates a biome of ghosts and memories, showing reverence to naturalism without confusing it for humanity or scholarship. Through precise imagery and radical lyricism, these poems reckon with loss and loneliness while carrying an urgency that feels immediate and universal."
JAMES WADE, Two-time Spur Award–winning author of *All Things Left Wild*, *Beasts of the Earth*, and *Narrow the Road*

✻

"At times funny and at times a gut punch, these poems weave image and language together to make us feel something. Habitats offers an ecological view to introspection, producing lines that cut to the bone while reaching toward nature, people, and memory."
CALEB COLLIER, Writer and co-founder of The Forest School and The Institute for Self-Directed Learning

✻

"Ashley brings the reader into close communion with the sometimes dignified and sometimes quirky world of southern forests. His voice is rich with melody, humor, and perception. This is a work to be read and reread with joy."
CAROLYN NEWTON, Novelist and author of *Songs of the Dead Road*

✻

"These poems remind us that trees are not abstractions, but nature's divinity. Ashley's surprising and brilliant approach to anthropomorphism recalls what poetry was meant to do."
DAWN MAJOR, James Dickey Fellow and poet, author of *The Bystanders*

✻

"Polyvocal and uncanny, these poems pulse with desire. Ashley invites readers into an interconnected world where trees summon the loved and lost, where understories are people and the wind is a bird."
WILLIAM WOOLFIT, Author of *Eyes Moving Through the Dark* and *The Night the Rain Had Nowhere to Go*

"In Ashley's work, the trees speak for themselves. This strange and pungent testament records sylvan voices with force and clarity. Reading these poems is an adventure you won't soon forget."

ANGELA BALL, Author of *Steeplechase* and *Afterlives of the New York School of Poets*, recipient of an NEA Individual Artist Grant

※

"Moving through the landscapes with exacting precision, Ashley renders each poem ripe with its own telling. These poems reward the act of witnessing, offering raw and necessary understories."

GLENIS REDMOND, Inaugural Poet Laureate of Greenville, South Carolina, and author of *The Song of Everything*

※

"Reading Garrett Ashley's poems, I feel thrown off balance in the best way possible: the familiar is made strange, the known southern landscape freshly engaged in a project of exploration and recovery. From the habitat of a particular tree to a gulf beach to a trailer to a grandmother's bedside, these poems ask us what we're dwelling on and dwelling in. Ashley's work is lyrical, haunting, and strangely comforting in its discomfort, as questing voices ground themselves in the heroic project of being fully human."

JENNIFER HORNE, Twelfth Poet Laureate of Alabama, 2017-2021 and winner of the 2025 Hall-Waters Prize for Excellence in Southern Writing.

※

"Garrett Ashley's lyrical and unflinching poems continue to follow me as I move through my own habitats and landscapes, asking me to think about my relationship to the natural world, the self, and others. In Ashley's poems the personal becomes ecological and historical, helping us to understand a little bit better what it means to be alive in a world that can be both brutal and beautiful."

ANDREW MALAN MILWARD, Author of I Was a Revolutionary and You Are Loved, winner of the Juniper Prize for Fiction and the Nilsen Literary Prize.

III *[Where We Live]*

As It Turns Out, I Couldn't Wait For Summer—67
The Piano (First Apartment Out Of Woods)—68
Bloodchild Lesson Plan—70
Brief Complaints About The Present Moment—72
Remember, Objects I—73
Remember, Objects II—74
Remember, Objects III—75
Not Seeing—77
Nostalgia—79
Mississippi 1996—81
Magnolia—83
The Chair—84
No Trailer Ever Can—87
Sink—88
Sometimes I'm Reminded Of Pale Insects
    Tossed Through The Air—89
Habitats—90
Bird—92
Stay—93

Acknowledgments—97

HABITATS

I
[Anomalies]

THE CLAMS

The Beach:
    The hole is deep, and contains a clam
    a shell made of brown organic material,
    hard, with a thick fleshy organic body
    poking out, hanging loose like a tongue.

    The act of clamming represents post-war mobility.
    Americans, a period of calm nothingness, and clams
    don't mean anything, unless nothing can be represented
    by the shell of a clam, its foot dangling in the air
    when lifted from the sand.

    The hole is covered, sand marked by a dimple,
    the clam two to three feet deep, waiting to be unearthed.

    Behind, an overcast sky
    foregrounded by boardwalk.

    The man looks across the beach for his son;
    adjusting the empty mesh sack under his arm
    returns his gaze to the sand, talks to himself,
    digs into the sand like an animal

Woman:
    She looks down at her husband, digging.

    She told her mother this man was going to be her husband

    the man's toes curled behind him ungracefully

    as he puts the weight of his doggish position on the then

she watches her son bend down onto his knees to
reach into the hole.
They watch as the boy struggles to get the clam
it doesn't work, not even with his fingertips.
Sand is pressed into his nostril and ear and mouth.
The boy gets down against the sand and flattens himself,
arm twists into the hole, face reddens against the pressure
of the sand,
contorting his body in such a way,
the whites of his teeth showing

Man:
> *His father*
> *burned alive in a car in Vietnam two months*
> *before coming home. They'd sent back three*
> *fingers and a crust of ear*

—At the end of the summer I got so despondent
I had to learn to enjoy reading because I
couldn't do much else. I wanted to go outside
so bad and I could hear the wind banging
against my window and I had a friend
who hit my window with rocks,
eventually he stopped coming.
You wouldn't know that kind of loneliness,
the shortness of breath, the size of my stomach
expanding—

The Beach:
> The boy's head has gone into the sand.
> Meanwhile the man is transfixed by the sight of the boardwalk.
> A bicycle hanging off the edge under the handrail,
> other children playing down below, his old friends swimming without him,
> left him on the boardwalk, post sadness,
> allowed him to grow fat and slump shouldered

Man:
> —There are things I never learned from books—
> The boy has sunk and only his legs show.
> His legs are like saplings
> twisting in the wind.

Man:
> —I had a bicycle but could never work up the nerve to go anywhere on it—
>
> the boy has sunk so deep into the
> sand he can no longer breathe.

Man:
> —I'm happy you don't have to know any of that—

VOICES OF THE DEAD

Don't go to the store,
   a voice said this against
much crying, teeth gnashing,
buzzing like an organ play.
   The store will be robbed.
   A car will sail through the glass and
   you will be standing there—
then I hang up on my mother,
we're left with the docks and seagulls nesting, and clams—
   burrowed in sand, within
   graspable distance. Clams of shimmering blue
   swirls on shells.

Mussels climb onto the docks: this one we're under
weighed down by men sitting on ice chests,
slender fish hanging from lines.
   "That was your mother," he says to me.
   We'd heard her voice together.
   Water runs over our feet.
Boys in coats chase one another,
crunching barnacles tender as
sugary glass. He gets up and wanders off
in an existential huff.

The afterlife is thinking of us.
Old men wearing rain jackets
shake their heads at seagulls.
   Someone on the pier
   asks about snapper.

      A girl stops to dig at something in the sand
        before looking up and seeing her father has kept
           walking,
      eyes scanning for holes.
Young people scrape up plastic bottles washed along the beach.
Farther up the shore, tufts of gray weeds break through sand,
push against sun-bleached clamshells.
      You tell him when he comes back:
      nobody knows anything about anything.

PINE MEMORIES

1
A blank-faced clock stands
against plywood wall, shows
sun weariness from years of
living in my father's garage
where it lay flat beneath the
window. We breathe its
sighs like fuel.

2
If that dog doesn't make a
sound, I'll scream. The wind
is padded, the limbs moving like
air against the window, creating
shadows through orange light,
feels padded. There is a sound
of engines on the highway, and
what was once a dog wet from rain,
matted, sitting open-eyed in my chair.

3
Have you ever felt eyes on
the collar of your shirt, pumping
gas at the Eagle Mart—these
people are no longer like you.
Their hair is music. And there are
trains left empty in yards: graffiti
bigger than a house, artists our
age having gone on to more things
else. Give one a chance to breathe.

4
A mountain's head is removed,
sliced away as though with a knife.
When you get the call about how
much these trees are worth, you
go home and cry and sift through
the refrigerator, try to take your
mind off pine needles as much as
you can: this death cold as
refrigerators, though permanent.

5
At this angle, the building looks
like an atom. Has a face on one end,
a trick of the light. What was once your
cheek pressed into glass, grease
stains now wooden doorways,
the vibrations of feet crunching my blue
padded floor. At this angle, the train
is the sound of a roar. And at this
angle, an arrow in space towards us.

PINE MEMORIES II

I know we were hemorrhaging
forgiveness and we've been through
this before with bloodred fingertips.
Pine needles in transition: brown
on a slope of earth on a farm that
doesn't feel displeasure in its stacks
of logs. Machines have come in and
caused too much damage. There was
a road here—see the way it bleeds through
like Cogon grass, nettles, yellow weeds.
You said, *Here's how to work it out.*
Make it stick this time. I believe you.
I know we want the warmness of cell
phones, invitations finally to one another.

We have pine memories like
such a pack of losers—remember
when there were geese in the
sky. We remember hemorrhaging
teeth and whale bone. We
remember digging holes in the
field and planting their tree
corpses there. Smell this for miles.
We come home in December.

DECEMBER

She was there with her brother, who wanted to see the park
    one more time.
She wasn't happy to be with him this way. People watched
    them as they

passed. But when he asked to sit at the bench she felt terrible
    for sheltering
        this unhappiness.
I can't believe I was like that, she later said over

drinks. And the later years: of gluing matches together in front
    of children,
grading their math homework—she did this at home when she
    might have

watched CSI: Miami or fallen asleep to art tutorials on
    YouTube; one night,
    her son called to say he was gravely upset about—but hold
        on—

it wasn't like her to understand something so deeply—please,
she wanted to say: I haven't even grieved my own, yet.

We were moving around a corner when we spotted them
    sitting
on a bench. The woman wore a blue jacket, her hair back in a
    ribbon.

He was hunched over, pale, his face looked down at the rocks.
The woman sang something into his ear,

but neither of us could decipher it.

※

A pine behind the house has a lean to it. The limbs on one side had been cut away
by someone else and I'm afraid if we don't get rid of it, it will fall on the house.

When the wind blows, it sways a little and drops

sticks and needles on the shed. The neighbor came outside and yelled
over the fence: "Look at that!" She pointed at the buzzards

sunning themselves on a limb. If they'd been a snake, they'd have bit me.

GHOST BALLOON

The idea of ghosts has made me color centric—
when I'm with other people, I find that I am
capable of naming over twenty trademarked

shades of blue, and I can will them to you spiritually
as if from a dictionary of color. Seeing my grandfather's
shadow, though, has made me feel more watched

than ever before: I could never argue with my wife
about the placement of furniture, grit my teeth in the
mirror, yell at myself for water

pooling into the laundry room. There's no place in
this house to hide. They watch from above. I don't
mean from heaven, but from clandestine balloons. Or

they hang from dead treetops, binoculars in hand.
As children we believe we are all special
like this, enough to be watched.

WATER NOISE

I can't make heads or tails of
wind curling over a still body of
water.

I can barely see
him now; leaping, a tall figure
with well-worn boots.

The drowned man had been shot by
police: he is there now holding the baby,
it's clear as day—this happened.

When I experienced my own drowning I
wore denim shorts; it was the nineties.

A hand kept me under: we'd been forced
into the water, six of us, in a grove of
pine trees,

the hand holding me down by the back
of my neck like the claw of a lobster.

It hurts me that denim is coming
back in style, and how nostalgia
is a trend

and not a disease
that smashes my nose with
rocks.

A boat speeds by and
doesn't slow down even though there's
a no speeding sign.

I've never looked into the
Pontotoc River and seen so much
trash after a storm.

SPIRITS OF NORTH AMERICA

My body hurts worse the closer I get.
Last month I stayed at the Dauphine hotel; the same week
I went to a theme park,
ate funnel cake and spent nearly a grand on
drinks   for myself.

Then a two-week break, tiredness setting in. My mother visits
    me;
She keeps her left eye closed
        Like I   remember.
Purple spots on her hands
from years of trimming the cartilage of wings.

She lingers in place
at the front door, lets the wind in.
        You hear the breath of someone
        in the room,
    see things with clarity now
that   you,   you know.

When I make my next
stop, the most famous haunted house in North America,
I expect something
other than tourists and the obligatory
     entry-level tour, our guides ready to go
     home   like you know.

What I'm looking for is life outside of expectation; I float
for the smell of basil, mustard seeds, and bitter

thyme. Now there are some drunk kids on the porch.

Yelling so loud that I go to confront them. *I'm dying,*
    I want to say. *Have you ever known anyone who's been dying?*

But before I say anything the leader steps funny off the porch
    and his ankle explodes like buckshot.

        They are gone now and I'm no more   thankful
        than I could have been had something really happened
        for me in earnest. I could listen for the spirits
until I fall asleep. I hope I can speak,
be spoken to.

ONE WAY I AM ABLE
TO REMEMBER MY MOTHER

I believed for several days my mother
was back in the house with me. We heard her at night,
      a whirring in the corner
      where she'd sat in her chair watching MSNBC.

We never got along. She called me fat most of my childhood
      and   before she died, she'd been
      difficult in other ways:

she kept spilling the medicine on the nightstand
      beside her chair.   She'd grab my hair and yank me.
      I fucked up so bad cooking for her
we resorted to baby food.   One time she handed me

a paper cup: when I looked inside there was a perfect
swirl of shit; she lay back down and would not even
watch television.

She said things that didn't make any sense:
there were people standing in the yard watching
the house (there weren't).

      She waited on people who'd been dead forever.
      my grandfather was coming
      home from his rig and would be bringing her
      to school this week.

I'd suppressed good memories of her:
We listened to Loreena Mckennitt and
The Cranberries on repeat. We made fun of the same
people in church: the woman in choir whose voice sounded
        like   gears grating.

we had the same small hands—
we never pressed them together but they might have
been a perfect fit.

The whirring turned out to be the guest bedroom's window unit,
which kicked on automatically, quietly
so as not to shake the whole house.

TRAPDOOR

Camping at night we heard soft footsteps,
ghosts of Confederates complaining in the
woods.

No, we imagined it having been told this
was something we might hear. We grew hungry.
We left and snuck

into one of the old war houses,
found bats no larger than my thumb hanging
from the bedroom ceiling. My friend

plucked one from the doorframe like she was
picking strawberries, and it flew
out the window.

I hit a bat, one time, with the car.
I was driving to pick up someone for a date,
and it's one of those things

I was never able to explain to her; no one
understands how the image
of a tiny mouth opening and shutting

like a trapdoor leaves an impression
on someone who's never seen anything
so small and barely alive—

I tell people this when they also have bat stories.

YEAR OF BASKETBALL

The wind is a surprise and stays with
us through summer, working at the
poplar trees until they bow, their tops
brown, perplexed in their tension. I'm
reminded of the wind as I shot basketball
on a busted court near an abandoned
shopping mall.

Weeds grew through cracks. It must
have been early in the morning because I had
a headache. I spent more time sitting
on the river gravel cement steps leading into
the pit of the court than actually shooting;
I don't know why I lied.

What do I recall here? The remnants of a
chain-link fence, a bird with raw feathers, sun
casting a filter of red. One day my friends
all disappeared. Recently I saw the trees
near the mall and they were bent in
the wind, fingers grasping like neurons.

SOMEDAYS I GO MISSING, AND GILLIGAN PRETENDS TO BE ME

1.
My name is The Skipper. I have a small hat,
and my best friend has a white hat. His
shirt is red like a flag, and there

are bags under our eyes as thick as
moons. We cry at night
like rabid animals. Doc says

we're going through a phase. But we
miss things in the form of
a vial of blue toothpaste,

sidewalks in the shade outside apartment
buildings, soaked wooden picnic tables,
the groan of cramped stomachs

after breakfast, waterlogged faces muddied
from staying out all night, nauseated
with a sense of an ending we never find.

Now our stomachs are full of sand.

2.
The first mate falls into the ravine again.
This time his shirt rips and
he swears into his hands and I,

The Skipper, retreat to my bamboo hut—
unsure whether I just heard *shit*, whether
there are voices in my head now from

the radio found in the lagoon by the Doc
in a frantic grab for civilization,
for want of love and love and love.

3.
The waves, miles out—
White lines against a procession of dark blue interlude.
Vegetables appear in the lagoon

and I, the Skipper, discover
Mary can see far off into the distance,
The white lines words of music, dialogue.

Mrs. Howell becomes lithe, a zip against time,
viewable via a brush of sand, footprints
with heated impressions, grains of light, and

the first mate has super strength.
I feel he could dash my head against
that rock over there and be done with me.

The Doc suggests my fears arise from
a thing I must have been promised
a long time ago and never got back.

For instance, when my father told me how

the ducks on the pond that flew away
would return. What return did he refer

to? I went home and discovered
the pond was dry and the house
had been sold and they had moved on

somewhere else; luckily, I had this
small boat which I could set sail on
and pretend things didn't just go away.

4.
A giant spider lived in a nearby cave.
We trained a pigeon to attack, but
the spider needed to be distracted

by a picture of itself and the Doc
tells me later—as we're both drinking
coconut rum—that this is the problem

with humanity. "We're trying to fit
too many things into one moment," he
says, dipping a finger into the rum, retrieving a fly.

We kiss beneath long nights of fitful sleep.
We dream the backseat of a Mustang,
envision a balding man with arms like palm logs

driving, this first look of happiness
since buying such an exquisite blue shirt,
these pants the creamy tile of a mother's kitchen.

5.
Somedays I go missing, and Gilligan
pretends to be me.

He puts on my spare hat
and scowls at our friends, saying:
"No one is the Skipper but me."

They go in search of me and when I'm found
sitting on a rock with a stick in my hand
thinking of nothing in particular,

I rip the hat from Gilligan's head,
a hot ocean pooling in my vision,
morning feeling, hazy, like home—

What keeps me going at night? I can't even recall
why I'm deteriorating against the side of this
palm tree. The sun feels good against my forehead.

6.
Last, we eat seeds which give us
questions and thoughts we shouldn't know.
We hate each other, hearing one another's

misconceptions—it's injustice in the blink
of our lips. Then one of us (not I, the Skipper)
gets the bright idea to burn the seeds

so we might love again. I look for credit where
nothing is deserved. The Doc says to
Gilligan: "For a guy who's always
doing dumb things, when you do

something smart, it's beautiful." The red of his shirt
noticeable from the sea, from the sky.

II
[A Field Guide to North American Trees]

AMERICAN HOLLY

Description:
Dense, like you know. When
my grandmother took me
to the skating rink I wore long
jeans which cast a spiny shadow.
My head is round and filled
with things, bright red
berries in a knot.

Leaves:
When my grandmother held
my hand she said I was like
holding warm leather, toothed
fingers, yellow green beneath
an onion-paper layer of god-
almighty thick elliptical.

Bark:
Like the rest of me: with a wart
which it was said was the result
of some amphibian peeing
on my skin (this could have been
a frog but I used to catch lizards
which would climb into my room
during thunderstorms). My favorite
memory, though, is when my grandmother
gave me a pine needle and taught me
how to fish for the insects living in
holes; drop the needle in and wait

for movement, and when you know it's
there, you pull with a great force but
not so much that it flings the insect
into the grass. I did this recently and
realized the brutality of it—

Twigs:
When my grandmother brought me
to get a haircut they all talked about
how fine my hair was and how
coarse it would become once I became
like my father.

Flowers:
We separate on trees. Short clusters
of us form to create new leaves. There is
always a base of which holds four
rounded white petals.

Fruit:
My face turned bright red when
my grandmother asked me to talk to another
boy about skating. She wanted me to learn how
to skate and make a friend. We mature in
autumn, a bitter taste in our mouths. This isn't
how we meet people, I wanted to say, except
I may be exaggerating my intelligence at the moment.

Habitat:
Wherever we are, it better be raining. There
are four degrees of weather: hot, with a bitter
edge, windy and of sawdust, and whatever
that thick feeling is when I haven't had
enough sleep. When my grandmother
came to wake me, I didn't even wash my
face.

Range:
Higher than I remember. Along the
Appalachian mountains; when—when
my grandmother remembered—the last time
I saw her I didn't know it was the last time
I would see her, and that's how things should
be, isn't it—when—

BALSAM POPLAR

Description:
Large tree with a bow. An
open space with uptight, narrow phalanges.
We feel one another in orbital crowns.
What is fragrant but the resin of our
Forearms—

Leaves:
Pointing at me, you know how
long ago. I have burrowed under you. We've
been jealous for years. You saw
my coffee mug and said, "That looks like
something I would have bought." Fair enough;
you know me better.

Bark:
Come visit me on this scaly ridge. I
have feathers where legs should be. This
is a dream, I say. But you swear you
don't understand, and I agree: you've
never known how to express yourself.
A dream is not something to experience
over a lifetime but a single night. It should
be hard and flat and forgetful—

Twigs:
Chromed; stout. Invite me to drinks
with your best friend. Tell me something I
haven't heard before. If I have to make our
dinner, eggs over rice with pepper again, I'll
cry—there are textures my teeth can
no longer bear.

Flowers:
There is one in the early
spring. There is one in the fall.
There is a noise in my bedroom closet I
can't decipher.

Fruit:
None; split into a thousand colonies.
Remember us together in a photograph.
Here is me on a speedboat, head pushed
forward, teeth bared; I wasn't thinking
about you or the process of wanting you.

Habitat:
I have lived in no less than
sixteen apartments. My age is written in my
hair and the carpet in my current home shows
signs of debilitating illness, layers of gray.

Range:
I have no range to speak. We
move and move and move and wherever
we are, we become rooted to the earth,
to the bone.

RED SPRUCE

Description:
The only spruce southward
of being described. We have eastern
hands. You said my face was
handsome. But I have a broad
forehead. People look at me and think,
"Oh yeah, that's one of those mountain
foreheads."

Needles:
Green, but not what you were expecting.
Sharp-pointed, all sides thin and with
the aspiration of leaf-likeness. I can have
whiteish lines. We saw a film, one
time, about two people living alone
in a spaceship, and we looked at each
other and sighed.

Bark:
We call movies films when we're feeling
haunted. We are haunted by trees and the
notion of reddish-brown familiarity.

Cones:
We hang in short intervals. We fall
straight, at maturity. We kill. We maim.
What are we even? Round pointed teeth—

brown with seed. Have you ever fallen
so hard that you made an excited thump
upon arrival? We do this to one another
one at a time.

Habitat:
We live where the rocks hang by a thread.
We long for some form of purity. I remember,
growing up, digging holes in the garden
where my father planted okra. I was looking
for the husks of dead beetles.

Range:
My grandmother once told me the best
home to find yourself in is the one
close to family. Don't move.
What's the point? You'll find something
here, trust me. That's what she kept saying.
She said one thing and looked away
when she finished her point; you never
know what they really mean. They
never look you in the eye when they're afraid.

JACK PINE

Description:
When people tell me they think
I'm wearing a wig, I spread my
arms and scream.

Needles:
Slightly flattened and irregular
to a fault. Trim your fingernails.
Hear that one aloud. When there are
no other people in the room,
do your sighs make a noise?

Bark:
Gray, brown with a hint of rivered
lines. I suggested to my therapist
that instead of tattoos, we should
etch music into our flesh so that
we can be played. And the therapist,
without so much as pausing to consider,
responded: "We'd need a mechanism
to travel across the world of our skin.
Records go in a circle." Another dream
ruined by people who are smarter than me.
Never say anything like that to me again,
I tell her.

Cones:
I stay here for so long it makes me sick.
I fatten. I worry over the size of my
midsection. I get a call from my mother
asking why I never send her pictures.
This is an old story, but I will tell her again.

Habitat:
If there was any place I could go
to be buried, it would be the sand.
It would be where a rock could
shade me in the afternoon. My head
would fold in on itself, and I would see
grains of sand imbedded in moisture—
my tongue would turn to sand.

Range:
Where there was an honest attempt
to make our organization better. The floor
manager, who knew network coding better
than anyone else, walked out, said she
was going back home to live with her parents;
her mother was dying. I felt some connection
to this. Our department went out to dinner
and I asked her: what can you do for someone
when they're dying? Take off work?
But the waiter came up
and she ordered a pitcher of beer for the table;
we—I never mentioned dying again.

GINKGO

Description:
Planted here with a mouthful
of age. When I don't have
flowers, my eyes wander. There
are mice at my feet. Mice waiting
for something that I can't give them.
My name means fragrance in
over seven dialects.

Leaves:
Without you. Without a turning
point, without remembering. We
have yellow in our hair. When
we came here, we were buried
in memory. When our names
were folded in paper, the paper
was dropped in the rain. I know
this is not the place to break down,
but look at me: green in twilight, all
veins. Don't laugh, thank you.

Bark:
Not becoming. Rough in the skull;
here is my mother's Bible. She
kept it in a drawer next to the bed
until she died. The family tree is in
there, she said, but when I looked,
the pages were missing. I'm sure
there is some adventure in this.

Twigs:
With or without you. *I like that you
lost some of your hair early on—*
that's the thing that's hardest to
convey, that what distances us
the most is what makes us human.

Seeds and Male Cones:
Not on me. Within the palms of others.
I came to the door naked and listened
as a car drove by. I wondered how strong
the wind must be before lifting a car
onto its side, tossing us into the ditch.

Habitat:
We can have a lawn, so long as
there is a fence. We watch for
holes at the bottom: when I was
a child, I remember the cat got
out and was gone more than a
week. I don't remember her name.
This should be important right?

Range:
All over. We got here by boat
and by sea. When I landed,
it was face first in the sand.
My face has taken so much
pressure over the years. When
we look at one another, we imagine
different people, times, places; you
tell me you like that my earlobes
show through my hair.

LIVE OAK

Description:
Ever green. A blanket
held against the base, we turn
into one of many. Long
branches,
a chord of ocean-bound fibers.

Leaves:
What one would assume—elliptical
and thicker than hell. I wonder whether
we fly straight
or if there is a new motion keeping
us to the ground.

Bark:
What dogs do. They hang around
waiting. Although I tried
to leave the house recently
and remembered that
I'd been charged with
taking care of my own child.
If don't run away now,
I might not ever.

Habitat:
If I don't run away now,
there will be a full-grown
person here beside me.
Things take time.

Range:
When I came from
Mississippi, I knew better
what to say about range.
My skin flakes in precision.
My brain is telling me
to "go this way,"
while my fist grips
toothpaste—it's
nearly that time again.

LOBLOLLY PINE

Description:
In an old field. Commercial,
Southern as Jesus Christ
with resin and bathroom
fragrance, the spread of even
arms and we don't see
these things anymore—on the
side of the road, a silhouette
against highways,
green oceans which occasionally
leap, scream as they are taken
to pasture.

Needles:
What we shout. A last bundle
before brown winter. Twisted
as though there was some reason
like I twisted my ankle just
stepping off the sidewalk.
Two cars drove by and I could tell
they were looking at me through
gritted teeth; nobody stopped.
Only thirty years old—what the
fuck—why does this happen?

Bark:
A black map, levels of an
encounter. Imagine driving a car
through this landscape like in

Baton Rouge where we looked for
the last house in the world for sale. We made
an effort. And imagine barking
at the moon, a crash in mind. We
were good while we lasted—

Cones:
We open at maturity. We dream
of falling on heads. A thump against
moist earth. To land on a head: that
would be bone-crushingly good.
We dream of killing, maiming.
A mother would recognize us, love
us, put us on shelves as her own
children. A cone is a method of
love and solitude.

Habitat:
From the deep. We were born
poor. Nobody recognized us
in flooded earth as children.
Try for a moment to remember
our abandonment. A helicopter flew
over the barn where we were hiding
and we dove into the hay.

Range:
All across. No longer native. We
are fast growing, and we see through
the bullshit of others. Remember
the sound of mud as your face enters
it, in the eighth grade, when you
were called—don't grit your teeth when
I repeat the words—I can't even say
them here.

POISON-SUMAC

Description:
Poisonous, narrow-heeled
with wax teeth: you remember I bit
your arm and you cried. Stood in
the yard with my teeth showing,
white like berries, all drama.

Leaves:
With you. Stems and feathers.
Once in flight. Red without.
Once without teeth, ovate—shining
once more. My arms have shrunken into
animal undertones. All this because I asked
if you would bring me autumn; drive
me to your place if only to hear the roar
of your car.

Bark:
My skin is not without blemish
but you can't see anything. This is what
matters: gray, thin lines. No holes. We
pretend what we want to see, only
there is no way to believe elsewise.

Twigs:
My hair turns gray at midnight. Otherwise
I am red; believe that it is red even
when it is gray at midnight. Holding me
in the closet, you'll notice a change in texture; it's

a lack of faith you detect, your own eyes
deceiving the inert part of you that detects
inertness.

Flowers:
I can be either: same or separate
in early summer, I change in longing.
My hair is only gray at midnight.

Fruit:
This is a secret: no hair. Numerous.
When others droop, I make clusters of
early autumn—this is the hardest thing,
describing something I'm not
even meant to know myself.

Habitat:
I like it wet. In the bog, and my favorite
word that has to do with wetness is
seepage: this word makes my skin crawl.

Range:
Don't fuck with me
anymore. A story: I was
going to my car one day and my shift manager
accosted me before I even had my keys in
palm like wolverine; car lights came on
automatically and my shift manager asked
about my weekend and I said "transforming
again, sitting on my ass, video games, etc.,"
when I should have told him all about a funeral
I was meant to attend but, as they say
> *If a bird lands on my*
> *Shoulder they are welcome.*

SWEETGUM

Description:
An aroma like grease, a year in bones.
Where are you, when will you be home?
A metal wheel and metal car parts hung
in the dirt. My grandfather could wiggle
his ears nearly to the top of his head. We
picked up trash underneath the sweetgum,
threw scraps into the back of his truck.

Leaves:
—he could hotwire a tractor with wires
underneath the starter button. His hands
were big and yellow in autumn, fingers
opened like stars.

Bark:
Deeply furrowed. Gray, and in the summer
red like Alabama clay. I asked him about the scar
on his chin—
he got it throwing knives at trees.

Fruit:
We fall, and parts of us rot away. We become
weightless and brittle in October. I pick at my nails,
imagine the stain at his fingertips. His ears
full of hair, the moles on his back sliced away.

Range:
My grandfather was a locomotive engineer with
Illinois Central; he knew how to be everywhere.
We would wait for him every day to come home,
the clock over the doorway framing the garage.
> *Any moment now, that door will open;*
> *we will hear his footsteps.*

LONGLEAF PINE

Description:
Neck like a candelabra. My bones show, this
psoriasis a patch of sun, my fingers
sharp, a spread of knives, a clutch of feathers. Not
even as bad as others have had it, my mother
says. Who felled you before? Who made
money from your limbs?

Needles:
A bundle of drooping dark green—moveable
objects are my body. Here is an impression
of falling apart: [my mother doing a shift
at Piggly Wiggly]—here is an impression of her
shadow [fingers on the wall, the form of her
sitting in a chair, head slumped to the side]—watch
as my fingers move to create the
silhouette of her face.

Bark:
Fire resistant; what is rejected at our feet
turns to seed. This is a controlled fire. She
tells me. Our skin remembers this. Understories
are people and the wind is a bird, is a bird—

Cones:
Like cannonballs, like unfolded umbrellas,
like a small prick. Catch me, keeled hands,
catch me or I will be the understory. I will
crush skulls, leave an impression of my nails—

Habitat:
Enslaved men reaped them, she says: their heads turned
to bark, licked by ash from the understories:
these trees are straight. How many men lay their hands
to the bark, looked up through Virginia, saw a cloud
that wasn't a cloud, a shine that wasn't a bird—

Range:
      —and imagined, like a bird, they could fly as well—

SLASH PINE

Description:
Narrow—my skull, a crown of needles
brittle as sugar. We have heads
of turpentine, are used up like plastic,
and slowly begin to feel the need to drift
somewhere else.

Needles:
Green, a bundle, an exploding start. Look at me
straight on and you'll see it, some starry silhouette.
If there were flowers on your dashboard, they would be
evergreen. We drive the car across the Florida
panhandle, get a motel facing the sand. Feels like
home, you say.

Bark:
Purple sky—a rim of sunburst cloud, a shelter
for motel sand. Sand in rivulets, my arms covered in
lines of it, sand in my mouth, between my teeth,
on the floorboard of the car, sand somehow
in the glove compartment, in the pockets of my
jeans, my arms, wind churned and my skin hardened
by the cutting sand.

Cones:
Just like everything else. Our leftovers,
what we forget on the sideboard of the hotel room—
a plastic bag full of snacks, a plastic comb,
hair ties, a house key, saline solution, a vial

of makeup (rolled behind the motel lamp out of sight)—
these things leave cone-scales on our bodies.

Habitat:
In the morning the beach was covered in thousands
of man o' wars. We picked them up with sticks
and threw them at one another. Panama City is a habitation
for alien life and the buildings here (like thumbs, like
fingers) at the tree line, are far from home.

Range:
Go back to Baton Rouge and taste the air,
windows down. Look for her there, where
she is buried. In bogs and church cemeteries. Her skin
like wax paper. Let her voice speak to you in
the highway wind:
      your hair looks a mess.

TREE OF LIFE

Description:
The last known photograph of God
was taken in Silver Cross Health and Rehab
Center's room 127. My grandmother leaned
forward to take one final look at me. Through
the window behind her, a tree reached
from heaven to earth. I can't see it, she told me.

Leaves:
We are dry year long; black veins grow
through us. She holds a handful of scars.
She weaves a basket of scars.

Bark:
Like lines, like liniments, a pattern, a
fabric contorting, falling upward back to you,
God: cover her knees. Shield the helix of her ears
from chill air.

Flowers:
God is a nurse with combed hair. God is
the empty vase sitting on this
Formica nightstand, the orange service light
over the swing bed. God is all flowers or
none, yellow and white and that color that appears
when oil runs through water. God is the scuff
mark on the floor, the smell of ammonia in
the hallway, the folded towels in the closet, the
water that stays pooled around the base
of the sink in the bathroom.

Fruit:
She hands me this, says *taste*—
but this not a pomegranate, much more
like beating heart, like nostalgia.

Habitat:
She has lived here her entire life. Has become
rooted to this clay. The tree outside the window,
incidentally, referenced before—that tree was
never really there.

Range:
When my grandmother died, I refused
to look at her body. Because I didn't want
to see how she changed after clinging here
so long. I do not regret this. She
is in good hands. If asked how I could believe in heaven,
I would say because she is there.

CRAPE MYRTLE

Description:
A web of fingers, spindles, clownish. But here they
come, those city workers, on the weekend before Spring.
I never know what they're doing, when it will be my time.
A bird writhes inside me. Underneath, a bed of pine
straw, fire ants, the remnants of my face (after a blast of wind),
which is her.

Leaves:
The city workers strike these fingers away. One
sits on the curve and wipes his nose.

Bark:
That was done too fucking short. But no matter
how many times we cry about it, they insist: fingers
are not meant to protrude this way; my skin is restricted by
this growth. Another worker grinds away:
his nose red as clover.

Flowers:
But that's not all, by God: my arms are removed,
thrown in the back of a city truck, and I am suddenly less—
I think of her, and I am less. I think of her as I lessen,
her face pink as my face.
And where birds writhed.

Habitat:
I am suitable for compact spaces. We
become more compact the more
we lose. Without this. Without this—

Range:
My head is removed. My neck, my shoulders. The more
I lose of myself, the less I remember. What was my
grandmother's name? I lessen, eventually
unrecognizable. I think of her face once more,
once more, once. She had ears like tea saucers.
I am less; I am less.

RED JUNIPER
(EASTERN RED CEDAR)

Description:
There is no better method of describing the aroma of lungs:
broad, sweet, exhale—night, buttressed, like homesick wood
after being split.

Leaves:
Scalelike. Have you ever heard this? With
eczema. With fibro. With gland-dot. Put me
behind your ear, let me separate your hair.

Bark:
Thin. Thin. Fibrous. Can you believe only
thirty years ago, my skin was not even my
skin? My spur instinctual, my hold on things
aggravatingly naïve. Sometimes, I imagine myself
young again: something spoken which I regret which
I hope nobody remembers. My lungs, broadening,
expelling more than they breathe.

Cones:
Dark blue; the hint of bloom; it occurred to me
today that I have never seen my insides.

Habitat:
Limestone; the swamp where my hat was thrown,
where I drank my first root beer on the water; abandoned

fields like where crows gather; on fence rows where I take
on an existential beauty (look at the way I sit here beneath
the crows, for the crows, still); scattered geographically.
I exhale more than I breathe; my family is of a world too broad
to name, call my own.

Range:
As long as I am here, I am anywhere.

AMERICAN SYCAMORE

Description:
Maybe what we see when we imagine
"tree." Unclear whether this sycamore is native
to the Eastern U.S.—there are sycamores
all over the world, and research is conflicting,
conflates sycamores of the western
hemisphere with those of the east
(the internet is unsure where the oldest
trees were felled). One of the largest
hardwoods, crooked, broad of crown.
Do we see this tree, when we look?
I am too tired to think about trees, now.
I am too tired to think.

Leaves:
Hairless. Imagine my hands, except
green. I have trouble understanding
how this is important, but some men
have hair on the backs of their hands,
hair that pours from jacket sleeves
like rats' nests. It also needs to be said
that I have never seen an apple tree.
It occurs to me, if I saw an apple tree,
I might be amazed by it—apple is one
of the first words we learn to spell, after all.

Bark:
White, unfurling. Slices of bark peels
revealing greens and orange beneath.

I have run out of energy, though—
most people, at the end of the day,
only want to come home and watch television.

Twigs:
Ring scars. Nodes, in the millions. There are only
so many ways to compare the hands, the fingers
of my grandmother to the hands of a tree.

Fruit:
My favorite line from the National Audubon Society
Field Guide to North American Trees, Eastern Region:
"usually 1 *brownball* hanging on long stalk,
composed of many narrow *nutlets* with *hair tufts—*"
when I get home, I clean the cat's litter box. I hold the cat
against my chest until he purrs. I fight bamboo in the yard.
I take a shower, moan existentially as I wash my arms. I crash.
Sometimes I almost call my grandmother.

Habitat:
Everywhere, apparently. In my backyard,
growing up. In fields beyond barbed wire,
beyond the crows there, among the forever.

Range:
Where do we move and why? Where
does the yard encounter field? All these
people with mountains in their yards,
up the street, picturesque: how well
do they see them anymore? Are they even there?

SOUTHERN MAGNOLIA

Description:
My grandmother looked out at the magnolia
from the bed in her living room. The leaves,
she said, were like parchment paper. If
I could climb the limbs just one more time,
she said, always with the accent of some
ghost or another.

Leaves:
Parchment, waxy, slick. She sleeps under
quilts, her bed full of pale undergrowth, a chicken,
some beetles, a plot of dirt marred with black.
She used to lick her fingers before turning
the pages of a book.

Bark:
The floorboards—from the hallway to the side
of her bed—squish when stepped on. Whereas
the skin of the magnolia is rigid, a pale
evergreen bone.

Flowers:
A legion of God. Cream colored
as the moon. Slivers of skin beneath
her eyes. What a smell—she holds
the petal to her nose, inhales the pistil,
ovule down to sepal, like morphine.

Fruit:
Sometimes I ask the dead: if you were here
today, would you recognize my voice? These
fruit scattered on the ground around the tree
remind me of cigarette butts; their red seeds
smooth like candy.

Habitat:
Moist soil of valleys. The wind shifting
in the memory of her gray hair. The wind
and the soil and the wind and her hair,
thinned, combed over,
weighed down by moths.

Range:
Blessed be the bird in your limbs. Blessed
be those who walk not in the counsel
of the ungodly, the misshapen horticulture,
the pointed-beaked shrub, the chainsaw. Look
how barren the earth has gone beneath
the magnolia, look how the leaves crumble
        when she sleeps.

III
[WHERE WE LIVE]

AS IT TURNS OUT, I COULDN'T WAIT FOR SUMMER

I barely remember you,
the hiss of bowls
holding

brand-named cereal,
a cord of yellow thread,
bodily

leading to oxidation
I recognized as a vault
except with

a face like you. I heard
a song—the climate like
dogs, children

listening to radios—I wish
I could feel the wind against
bare legs.

Your voice the brush of pine
needles, water, something
unidentifiable.

THE PIANO (FIRST APARTMENT OUT OF WOODS)

1
A very loud truck drove by. It frightened the birds in the grass beneath my balcony.

2
Its engine stuttered at the four-way light. I could hear it all the way from my balcony before it lit again in a blaze of exploding pistons.

3
A loud truck drove by today while I was drinking coffee. I barely had any sleep last night. Some birds were on the power line by the Shell station. I could see them from my balcony. They were unfazed by the loudness of the truck.

4
A loud truck drove by and pumped one for the boys. The hair of our necks lifts, that chemical feeling like heat spreads from our chests.

5
A loud truck drives in the direction of the school. There it will be with its friends, attend classes, complain about a core curriculum it is forced to take, which, well I don't know how to explain it either, and that's why I will never be a real educator.

6
I got up in the middle of the night and made coffee. My mother's piano sits right by the door. The house smells of coffee and I'm unable to cope with the fact that I will never learn piano, and the piano is too heavy for me to carry everywhere.

7
A very loud truck woke me in the middle of the night. I got up and took a shower and read a book for the first time since moving here. I don't even like reading books anymore. My mind kept saying: "I don't even like reading," and I read the same three sentences over and over.

8
A loud truck has a name. "Larry just drove by," I say to myself whenever I hear Larry driving by.

9
A loud truck crashed through the glass door of a Publix. Unstoppable, the truck made a hard right into the produce section, splattered a square display container full of watermelons, and finally came to a stop as it hurled itself onto the deli counter. Eleven people were killed.

10
A loud truck wakes me in the middle of the night. But I was having another one of those dreams, and now I feel safe.

BLOODCHILD LESSON PLAN

Not related, but talk about
how everything goes back to
Modernism.

Show Kadinsky's
accidental masterpiece,
"Sketch for Composition II,"
the one with the golden circle,
discuss the Modernists'
early as they say in academics

attempt to break away from
Realism—which is practically
devoid of humanity—I read
this somewhere but don't
understand it myself—

in order
to create outlets for artists
to explore some bullshit
or another, and play

in fields of grass, flowers and
with symbols and metaphor,
rather than attempt to tell
a story.

Cut your finger on the piece
of metal under the podium.

These authors might
have tried to interpret something
or another, interpret the grill
casing of a 1974 Buick.

Then speak about Tony
Morrison. *Sula*. Then read

aloud. Some Butler comments
at the end, barring time.

You are beautiful; your face and eyes
and deep voice; you are someone
with whom we miss.

You died before I knew who you were.
You were here a long time before
There was even—

Don't forget to talk about what you
came here for. Look out the window,
see trees swaying in the overcast sky.

BRIEF COMPLAINTS ABOUT THE PRESENT MOMENT

[your hair is
different and maybe it's because

of the crippling depression so many
artists seem to be referencing

in stories about reconnecting
with nature, whatever [. . .]

now and you claim to have never
seen an icicle before today. That's

not what I expected]

a tree is a crippling noise
in the bloom. That's a

rose opening in me: canopies
of birds, catching the sound

of trucks and Kohler trenchers
and sticks of cowboy dynamite

REMEMBER, OBJECTS

We zoomed down the hallway, arms outstretched
for some other place to hide. We got into
dark corners and held our breath, crawled
under the couch. Musty quilts drifted over us
like spiderwebs. My mother said we wore ourselves out
going like this.

You don't want to be a teacher, they said to me. This is
what you'll do to make money [they show me]; this is
what you do to get your shit together [they try to explain
what this means using the stony texture of their palms].

My father, who walked in his sleep, went into my
mother's bedroom and shot her ear off. When he came to
my bedroom, I was hiding. I didn't see him, and we
barely spoke after that—it's been years, which only
feel like a few months at best.

One thing about fathers: they were never hard to forget and
they left solid objects to hold and anthropomorphize.

REMEMBER, OBJECTS II

My mother took us to get groceries one day and I
saw you. I pushed you into the cart handle and you screamed.

I have no idea why I did this. My mother spanked me
next to a cardboard wagon full of tomatoes.

※

Years later, riding the boulevard I saw you on the side
of the road. Your window was up. I should have stopped

to see if you needed anything, but I couldn't recall the last time
    we spoke:
we were at a funeral, I think. I was trying to convince you

to test the cake. Your daughter was there, and her
mother, and I think you were trying to hide from everyone

because you did not believe you were the father and your
mother took pity on the girl and kept her, and you felt
something unusual about all of this—

※

There might be a cure for nostalgia. I thought social media
might be it. You'd eventually message back, and I don't
know why, but I felt a sense of gratitude.

Come to another funeral, you said. Come to another
showing of the body. But I can't anymore. I don't say this, but
I can't anymore.

REMEMBER, OBJECTS III

When I was old enough, I went in to treat my nostalgia. I was given a series of hallucinogenic drugs, asked to look at AI rendered photographs depicting a new park I lived by.

I described my current apartment; my favorite restaurant still in business; the smell of my favorite shampoo. This went on for months and I thought it was too late—
    my teeth were falling out.

My head filled with cotton. I began to have outlandish dreams of the park, my house, my favorite restaurant, and shampoo. But the park was still there; it had a bench, some gravel looking down a hill,
    some pine trees.

The restaurant was small, and people had written their names on the walls and columns, and a celebrity athlete visited, made the place even more popular. His picture hung on the walls.
    My apartment was empty—

a woman had lived here for several years and left stains on the carpet. There was something about the place I began to long for when I left. I dreamed about
    the apartment running away from me.

One day the dreams stopped. I barely ever thought of you
and never looked at old photographs. Sometimes
when I jerk awake at night, I go back to sleep,
having near enough forgotten—

NOT SEEING

1.
When the trees came down, I followed
you to college and didn't think much
about what was missing, so I spent the
next ten years trying to figure out
what I was good at.

You put on a hat made of paper which you said
was a list of all the things you never got to
do before you died of whatever it is that kills
people in poetry. I still dream of carrying
your corpse up a mountain.

Halfway there the casket is dropped, and your body rolls
onto soot, and something about the shape
of your face doesn't look right. This is
my metaphor for nostalgia: the first great
loss, maybe, being the trees,

not knowing it was about to happen but coming home
and seeing so many gaping holes in the
earth like downed satellites. And how I didn't
immediately register the empty space where
the trees had stood.

There must be some
psychological term for not seeing.

2.
When a healthy tree falls, it may take up the entire
root system like when we hold onto something we no longer
need but which we cannot live without.

3.
The other morning, I was
about to call my grandmother and that's how I realized
I'm not only nostalgic, but forgetful too.

NOSTALGIA

is a leg dragging behind
a limb like
magic invisible weights

which like you know
like a tree
without limbs poking

out of a perfectly
manicured lawn
like a needle

nostalgia is one more arm

hanging from beneath what functions—
ghostly nerve endings make wind
unusual—I drag this arm into
the store and at the register, heavy
basket hauled up to the conveyer
belt, one of the clerks ask whether I need
help and I say no
thank you, except when I get home
that night, I lay in bed remembering
his face, blinking my eyes in the dark
to try and imprint his face there

nostalgia is like this dead arm
I've removed despite
my doctor's plea
to never do anything on my own like that—

I throw my arm over
the fence into the woods so I
would never see it again

nostalgia was a dead arm still

attached, it hangs around like a stoned
kid. I don't even understand the
meaning of the imagery. Maybe
some years ago—if I could think
hard enough I would have this pine-
scented memory of what poetry
meant—

nostalgia, a dead limb carried
around as if in a
dream whose voice
comes only in a whisper, and
there is the anticipation of a shout: three
loblolly pines standing in a field in chromatic
light, the sound of heated wind
like

      hair drifting over paper,
      we have cement in bags, a basket of
      deformed fruit and dry lips
we breathe like we invented
      the very act of breathing.

MISSISSIPPI 1996

One story that has always given me trouble was about a boy who used to urinate on bathroom walls. I've tried fictionalizing this to make it manageable or to provide some kind of morality lesson or

something but I don't know. 3rd or 4th grade, and they were trying to figure out who was peeing on the bathroom wall. This went on for several months. We used to play at the edge of the woods

against the chain-link fence. We dug for insects / we crossed over the creek using a sewage pipe about a foot in diameter—I have dreams of a treehouse in that same spot, some large

bipedal creature living there waiting to strike, to see me poke my head up, maybe a metaphor for an increasing distrust in adults, the fear of the unknown. When we came in

from recess one day the principle was standing there in the hallway with a hand on the boy's shoulder, and he proclaimed that we had finally figured out who was peeing on the walls. He

asked us to stay, because he had to explain something very important to us, and this is the part
that is the most difficult to write not because I've been traumatized (this is not my story after all)

but because the leap from urinating on walls to homosexuality feels so abrupt that it has to be made up—his voice like a stone wall, like eggs breaking in a metal pan, like ground coffee—

Don't be like a faggot and pee on the walls, that's a thing I always remembered about that period of my life and I realize I don't even know the kid's name or whether he's okay now,

other things I remember would be pine needles brushing against an open sky—we were lifted by the heat at proceeding breaks, and the tree line surrounding us were robust of hair, with brown

spots mixed with the green and their canopies so far away that it felt like beyond the scope of a dream to touch them, to be with the pine canopies, to be up there away from everything.

MAGNOLIA

I sent you a message recently to the effect
of "Do you have a PS5? I can't remember
if you have one," and really I didn't care
one way or another if you had a PS5, but
my job in that moment was to wait
for you to respond and know that you
were still there in a similar place
and not as I imagine sometimes when
I dream of you climbing yet another magnolia.

There are two trees you climb in my memory:
one you get up quickly and one where you're
stuck at the midpoint and ants are crawling over
your arms, and you are afraid of falling.
The first tree is knotted, and sits on the
edge of the woods within view of the house.
I smell the pool from here. She is listening
to a rock station in the garage and suddenly
and maybe for the first time in my life I
recognize the hot chemical feeling in my
chest that goes by no name but which would
require so many other chemicals years later to subdue.

The second tree has a squirrel's nest at the top;
that was your goal. The nest as it turns out was
full of ants. I recalled this not long ago when I
was watching the news again. More bodies pulled from

the snow in Texas. I'm not sure what the correlation
is, my justification for asking if there was
some need, some fortress, a piece of earth
stuck in place.

THE CHAIR

1.
The river is quiet except for the faint
question of a voice on the
floor above me. It is cold.
*Did you just want to talk
or what?* A large, round stone
hits water.

2.
We came here just as
everything opened. The
tunnel smelled of crabs,
you sighed when
two people stood there at
the gazebo. We had never
met until tonight.

You looked different than in pictures.
you asked me about politics maybe
to catch me by surprise. There
were, you said, prerequisites to
love, sex, even just being.
The wind blew

behind the river pine
silhouetted night. What
did I say about politics?
"I watch the news. I draw hateful
images of Ron DeSantis in a notebook
which I keep on my chair."

3.
You asked about my
chair. How long I sat in it
when I came home, whether
it was covered in fur from
the cat. Whether I had spent
a lot of money on the chair.
I get attached to objects
like they were people.

Yes—me in
a nutshell, a chunk of gray cement ruptured
like in a dream like in oil.

NO TRAILER EVER CAN

Outside the trailer, in the rain, multiple people
look into the living room
with modular telescopes. The rain turns into hail and
they leave.

There are three fish in the pond.
My hands are cracked from the cold
and my lips hurt. The tree line behind the pond doesn't
belong to anyone.

A dog was stuck underneath the steps. The steps are
wooden, rotted, turning green. The dog was
trying to get to the chicken, had barked all day
and finally got the courage.

These people don't know what's happening
on the outside.

This is just a fact: a single-wide trailer costs about
forty grand more than it did ten years ago,
maybe this has something to do with the economy
of love.

When we look out of windows, knees on
couches, we eventually go away.

Someone out there pulls up,
it's so bright it's hard to see, we can't
even breathe.

SINK

Most people live in these conditions. Waves
of them like oil in water sloshed

around and we're trying to find just the right
stone. This reminds me of the way I rinse my thermos,

I swirl it around gathering as much soap as I
see and hold the cup under running water.

Gallons are wasted like this. I've heard
that most people live like this. A silence

only there in our hands, a triangle
of ceramic smoother than river rock.

SOMETIMES I'M REMINDED OF PALE INSECTS TOSSED THROUGH THE AIR

they remind me of fingers lopped off with
a hatchet, flicked underneath the table. These insects, an inch
long or more, versatile,
visibly brutal though I can't say I've ever been bitten yet, grab
ahold of the pine needle.

you see the needle wiggle and
you've been told all about
patience but you jerk the needle away like
a fishing line.

the insect is flung into the grass somewhere;
it can't return to its hole.

and
maybe this will have some kind of profound effect on you
socially/emotionally one day.
When I think of loss there are muscular cramps,
that urge to hold my own body lovingly,
to keep something growing that has already gone.

HABITATS

1.
A curtain is less than a curtain—beyond being
eyelashes, like underwear: there is a study
showing how twelve-thousand spiders make their
home in a single curtain in its lifetime.

I have lived in so many places
my thumbs are rough with curtain wear.

2.
I caught the neighbor in his yard yesterday morning, had
a Frostian interaction about putting up a fence.

I'm suffering from insomnia. The raccoons
in my yard bang on pots all night, but nothing
bothers me as much as the fact that I can see my neighbor
walking in their own yard, minding their business.

I ask if he wants to go in halves on a fence.

He pretends to like me and views my pot-beating
raccoons as a method perhaps of not needing to contribute
to the privacy fence.

3.
And beyond this I'm seeing gray on my head like
Tony Sirico. When I heard he died I looked at my
hair and brushed it behind my ears. I've had long

hair now for years and I've only cut it
once for an interview; beyond this no one has
said anything about it aside from the occasional you look like
Jesus bullshit, but it's not like they used to say
when you were a kid: *Cut your hair short for the interview.*
Look nice. Iron your clothes or you'll
become contaminated.

4.
I've been hiding this cat in the rental for three years
and I'm pretty sure the landlord knows, but they're
not saying anything because they know what a shithole
this is, anyway. Mold on the bathroom ceiling,
in the ventilation; exhaling its breath in the kitchen
pantry, snakes under the floorboards living within
grottos of mold. If I'm so used to
leaving, there's no reason for me to stay.

5.
The last place I'll live may be the rainy northeast.
There are romantic feelings swimming in my chest
about fighting the weather, overcast skies, falling in
love again in my seventies. People live way the hell longer
now than ever before. I'll need something to do.
Envision this: a towering rock over the beach,
unclimbable because I'm no longer a child. My knees
like marshmallows. I wear shoes that help with
blood flow. I bought these binoculars because
I always wanted a pair, but I see nothing,
fogged glass, and my eyes hurt. When I go back home
the binoculars will go back in a drawer and crack
when they feel me walking, my vibrations to them
like a train, some kind of avalanche.

BIRD

Ratty curtains catch the wind
a bird

comes inside and gets trapped. The tiny bird
flaps its wings in the corner of the room.

My unformed mind will never

forget how frightened it sounds, how
beautiful the blur of its wings

how lost its eyes how

silvered in my last,

how I imagine it
—until it flies

out the window and I know
this will be gone forever

STAY

Please do everything you can do remember this: the curved tree where we broke out in hives. This is the curved tree where you fell and skinned your ankles all the way down. This is the downed pine where it rained and you drew a shadow. This is the downed pine where you hid and ate persimmons. This is the bedroom where you lay awake listening to footsteps in the attic. This is the bedroom where you fell and broke the chair on the way down. This is the gravel pit where you nearly died of heat exhaustion. This is the gravel pit where you were first touched, boy your age not even old enough to know what he was doing, and you wonder now about that family, what happened to them other than cigarettes and drunken nights on Hurricane Lake—This is the apostle of despair; This is the apostle which led you on crying benders: cry holding this television remote, cry with your head against the wall, cry with this book open and your mouth dry as sand. This is the bathtub you nearly drowned yourself in learning to bathe; This is the bathtub you fell in like an old person because the knocking on the walls wouldn't stop and there wasn't enough time in the universe to have just this one moment; This is the stump that was once a tree where birds cried. This is the stump where you witnessed your mother pulling too fast out of the shed, gravel flying, rear-ending the brick façade running alongside the trailer; This is where you broke your toe on the hearth; This is where you lay down and watched the birds singing. This is where you'll believe anything; This is where you'll believe anything so long as it's coming from the mouth of someone letting you stay.

ACKNOWLEDGMENTS

Work in this collection has appeared in the following journals:

The Clams: *Tilted House*
Pine Memories: *Gleam*
One Way I Am Able to Remember My Mother: *Summerset Review*
Somedays I Go Missing, and Gilligan Pretends to Be Me: *Redactions*

LOBLOLLY PRESS

Loblolly Press is an independent press based out of Asheville, North Carolina that is dedicated to publishing contemporary poetry, short fiction, and novels from emerging and marginalized writers across the American South. Our goal is to publish writers with a distinctly Southern voice from communities and experiences not always represented in traditional publishing. We're striving to create a community of writers and readers who feel deeply connected to the work we publish because they can see themselves represented within it.

RECENT AND FORTHCOMING FROM LOBLOLLY PRESS

If Lost   Clint Bowman (2024)

Distant Relations   Cheryl Whitehead (2025)

Beasts of Chase   Andrew Mack (2025)

The Computer Room   Emma Ensley (2025)

Proud Roads   Kelly Riedesel (2025)

Preludes & Other Poems   Earl J. Wilcox (2025)

Habitats   Garrett Ashley (2026)

Of Water Never Ceasing   Kristin Entler (2026)

Slow Fire   Spencer K. M. Brown (2026)

Headings set in Warbler. Text set in Cormorant.

www.ingramcontent.com/pod-product-compliance
Lightning Source LLC
LaVergne TN
LVHW061619070526
838199LV00078B/7343